Joie de Vivre

The formula to enjoyment of life

by Alain Rheault

authorHOUSE®

AuthorHouse™
1663 Liberty Drive
Bloomington, IN 47403
www.authorhouse.com
Phone: 1-800-839-8640

Published by AuthorHouse 11/29/12

ISBN: 978-1-4772-9232-7 (sc)
ISBN: 978-1-4772-9233-4 (hc)
ISBN: 978-1-4772-9231-0 (e)

Library of Congress Control Number: 2012921723

Joie de vivre is a French term.

Joie de vivre is enjoying life to its fullest
and embracing what life offers.

Introduction

You can enjoy life and be happy. That is your choice.
Ladies and gentlemen, my name is AlainD.Rheault

Living life with Joie de vivre

This is a saying that I have created and want to share with you. *Joie de vivre* is being entirely comfortable to be your authentic self, to be grateful and at your happiest. It involves the moments you can truly savor, knowing that you listened and trusted the love in your heart—all the love in your life. It's having full faith in yourself and being the best that you can be. It's knowing you can trust your heart to live well with the solid relationships you have established with your authentic self and with others. It's knowing you have done your absolute best. It's living with no fear and with absolute joy, going after exactly what you want, fully enjoying the journey of your life and living in the present—this very moment—because you know life is beautiful.

When you know, who you are, you will know what you want. And when you know what you want, you will have the joy of living—joie de vivre. And truly, my friend, that is what a joyful life is all about—being happy with yourself and being able to choose what makes you truly joyful. Once you are happy, truly happy, you can help others be happy.

It seems that we want everything right now and forget about the journey of life. We want the results right now. Just take a breath here and start living your life. Enjoy the real quality of your life. *There is a map inside you. The feelings you have are your map. In fact, your life is easy when you follow what is inside your heart, when you go with the flow of your feelings. That is your quest; it is the journey that you have created. There is a time in your life that you realize you want to live the life you want. You have to go on the quest that you have chosen.*

It's my hope that through this book you will see what life can offer and really enjoy living it. That you will feel energized and feel good about yourself as you reflect on what you want in life and go for it one step at a time, one goal at a time. My intention for this book is that it will serve as a reminder of basic manners we were all likely taught at one point in our lives but sometimes forget to put into practice. It's my hope that you will have more fulfillment and enjoyment as you help others and look at your surroundings and environment with optimism.

We all want the best, to have the best, and to be the best. We all want to be able to really enjoy our lives and want others to be part of it. We want to love the things we do and the ones we share our life with. Remember how it made you feel. As I wrote this part of the book, I felt really great, genuine. I basically wrote this part for you, so you can ask yourself questions and feel the magic recipes inside this book. I want you to feel the answers of living the feeling of joy. Every day is a new day untouched; it is up to you to make each a good one. Realize you have the choice in life; it is all up to you, my friend. One of my favorite pieces of advice is this*: **B**e true to yourself. Enjoy every step of your life.*

Be 1 kind

Don't just be kind for the sake of kindness or how it makes you look. Be kind because you want to, because it can make a difference in someone's day or life. Being kind is not only beneficial to others around you—the little elderly women who you held the door open for or the complete stranger you bought coffee for. It really does bounce back to you. It's amazing how good being kind to others can make you feel. Be courteous to others; help people in every way that you can. Smile at everyone you meet, say hi to others with a smile, and listen to what others have to say. Be sincere.

Go ahead, open doors for others, let others merge in front of you during rush-hour traffic and give that hard worker a generous tip. In the end, you're being kind to yourself—while helping others in the meantime.

When you do things, do them all with the best of intentions and to the best of your knowledge and abilities. Be proud of helping, especially if you help without expecting something in return.

The object is not to give things or money to others; it

is the quality of the time you spend that counts. It is the feeling shared.

But when we think of being kind, we often forget to be kind to ourselves. I don't mean we should constantly splurge on ourselves and be self-absorbed or indulgent. What I mean is that we are sometimes quite hard on ourselves and don't always acknowledge our achievements—while we praise others for similar actions or accomplishments.

Remember to reward yourself for things you would reward others for. You got an A on your exam, you had a great job interview, or you finally got around to achieving a goal you had set for yourself. So go ahead and reward yourself—you deserve it!

Always be sincere about giving. Smile at yourself every morning in the mirror or when you glance at your reflection during the day. Be real; don't be afraid to be yourself. Don't pretend to be someone that you're not, because the only person who knows deep down who you are is *you*.

Live your life. Don't live it through someone else's eyes. When you have that feeling that you really know what you want, that is *you*, my friend. All you want to be is *you*.

You know you have dreams. Listen to you inner self; you know it's right when it feels right, because it feels good. It is all you when you take that time and listen to your self. Life feels good. Take good advice. It's for your own good to be able to help yourself and others. Allow yourself to *truly* be who you are.

Live your life the best way you can live. Be the best that you can at everything. Be true. Your true life is the energy in you. It's also in the things around you and the people around you. Feel that powerful energy!

Hurting others will likely hurt you just as much, if not

more. Your conscience is *powerful* and doesn't let you off the hook easily. *Do not* underestimate it. So, in hurting others, you also hurt yourself. That sounds like self-abuse to me.

Remember, being kind to others is also being kind to yourself. Be kind; don't purposely hurt others. Remember, it's a small world. Who knows, maybe the person you were just obnoxiously rude to might be the one across the desk from you at your next interview.

So, this brings me to my next reminder, my next question to you on positive thinking and life reflection: *How do you want to live your life?*

Live life and remember it all

Cherish the good and positive moments. Forget the bad and unpleasant moments. You want to feel good so keep the good. What do you want to do today? Make a list of things that you have to do and do them well. That is a big step toward your success, and you will feel great when you have accomplished what you had to do. How do you want to live today? That is the question you should ask yourself, because then you are choosing what makes you joyful.

You don't have to think long or hard about this, because you know what you want. You already know what you want today and already know what you want for tomorrow. You have to remember to *enjoy life*.

When I say this, I don't mean spend money or splurge on expensive items. To enjoy life, you don't have to spend money. All you need to do is observe simple things—like the sky. Look at each cloud. And take a few minutes to smell your surroundings. Smell the flowers. Bend down and put your nose in that fresh bloom and really enjoy it.

When I was little, I would watch my dad. I watched his every move. I thought, *I will be just like him one day.* Everything that he did, he did with the dignity of a real gentleman. My dad was really a perfect role model.

Almost everyone loves their dad. A good father always takes care of you. He has your back and you feel like everything is okay. My dad was a great carpenter. Everything he built was the best. He took pride in his work. He also took good care of his tools. He wrote his name on every one and painted the handles red, his favorite color. When he built anything, he made absolutely sure that the wood was straight and in good shape.

One day, as I was driving to work (I travel a lot and have long drives), I saw a very clean, shiny, well-kept *red* truck carrying a load of brand-new wood. This made me think of my dad, and I felt that, if he was to have a truck, that would be the one. So I waved to the driver. That, my friend, really made my day. It made me think of my dad. When it was time for me to buy a new truck, I bought a red one. Papa, I always want you to be proud of me, because I am proud of me.

It's not the objects or the material things that create a bond with someone. It is the time well spent; it is the interaction you have with another that counts. Take time for others and rejoice in every little thing. It is so worth it.

So smell that flower in front of you. Take the time to crouch down, touch the grass, and feel its texture. Touch the sand; feel it between your fingers and between your toes. Look at the moon and allow yourself to ask questions like, *Who else is looking at the moon right now?*

Really enjoy what you are seeing, hearing, feeling. Who are you sharing all of this with? And how do you feel?

Enjoy your surroundings. Describe them to yourself.

Listen to nature. Look at this *amazing* world we are all living in.

The answers you need are in your heart.

Take time to listen to your heart. Just take a moment right now and envision what you really want in life. Be really happy if you are living your dream. Can you see anyone smiling? Can you take time to share your smile? On your way to work, do you feel good? Better yet, on your way home, how do you feel? Is it a good feeling? Even though we all live pretty busy lives, can you stop for a moment and ask yourself, *Why am I in a rush?* Do you have time to give a hug or to pay a beautiful compliment to someone? We all want this but we easily forget the things that make others feel good, especially you.

Your success

Now, this brings me to the question of **Success**. What is it truly? What does it truly mean?

Success in life is doing what you *dream* of doing—becoming who you love to be and living up to who you say you are. It is the goal that you choose to accomplish, the goal that you want to achieve. It is the love and time that you put in, the sweat and the perseverance. It is the passion you apply to that goal. The more involved you are, the better the reward. I guess you could say that success is your reward to yourself.

It seems like the harder or more difficult a thing is, the better the reward always seems to be. That is because you put in more effort—or all of your effort. That is why you can really appreciate the reward.

So, my friend, be proud of who you are. Be confident in yourself; you are who you believe you are. Are you who you want to be? Are you convinced?

Have a vision of what you want to be. For me, the meaning of life is to live up to the vision of who I am and who I want to be. Live up to become what you have envisioned. But make sure what you really want is good and real.

Release all your energy, Walk with a purpose in mind. Walk with a full-of-life attitude. Be proud. It's all up to you. What is it that makes your heart beat and what makes you smile?

Success and well-being mean healthy actions, good behavior, and good motives. Success involves the way you think about yourself, the way you walk and present yourself, and even the things you eat and drink.

Most of us already know most of this stuff. But sometimes it helps to be reminded of factors that help improve our quality of life. Ask yourself, *Do I practice good manners? Do I treat others the way I want to be treated?*

Some of these important little positive things in life—no, *all* of these little things—are very useful for living at peace with yourself and with others. Sometimes a simple little comment, positive or negative, could have a great impact on someone's day—or life. You might as well make it a positive one rather than one that's potentially toxic to someone's day. Being negative bounces right back at you, which puts you in a bad mood, causing negative thoughts and escalating to bad habits that cause you to become a person I'm sure you don't envision yourself becoming. So, tell me, is it worth it?

If you have to do something, do it with pleasure. Do it with a smile. If you don't feel like doing it, wait a little bit; when you do feel better about it, do it and do it well. Don't do anything halfway; finish what you started. When engaging in an activity, do it to the best of your knowledge and ability. It's quite rewarding to look back on a job well done.

Sometimes things sound good—almost *too good*. If you're not sure about certain things that may seem too good to be true, talk with someone you would like to see yourself becoming or someone you trust, and seek his or her advice.

It's important to know what you want in life so when opportunity knocks you, know whether to take it or not.

It's much easier to focus on a goal when you know yourself and when you truly know what it is that you want out of life. Everyone wants the perfect life. So, what is perfect? Your life is really the life that you make it.

What makes your friends happy is not necessarily what makes you happy. Some people are happy with fame and others with fortune, while others may be happy simply when they are surrounded by people they love. When you recognize what makes you happy, you can focus on doing activities or even creating a business out of your passion in life. Work doesn't always have to have a negative feeling; try incorporating positive aspects into in.

It has been said in a number of books that *your thoughts create your life.* Have the attitude of "I can do it," "I can achieve it"—and really believe it. Surround yourself with the best of everything and aim to become the best. Have that certitude, that confidence in yourself.

If you know and think of the things you want, by working and taking action you make it happen. Doing what you really want to do and loving it—*that's* life. You can become who you want to be; it's really all up to *you* to make it happen. Don't procrastinate; find the time and do it. You know you've got the time. Your world is a reflection of yourself.

There's no competition; it's your own life, no one else's. When you are at work, be a good worker—not just for your boss but for yourself. Be proud of your work and always try to be better than you were yesterday.

What is important to you?

Be mindful and aware of your surroundings. In other words, don't just look at your environment, *notice it*. Really allow yourself to be in the moment.

You know that there are lots of different types of trees, but try noticing more: observe the leaves, the trunk, and the variety of colors during fall. Notice the sky; notice how the clouds never have the same shape and how unique each one is. Notice your environment and how you are part of it.

Look around and notice people. Open your eyes to recognize the ones who truly need your help. Also welcome people's compliments. When someone gives you a compliment, take it in. You're worth it and they mean it. Many of us tend to brush off a compliment, maybe because we do so out of habit or maybe we are trying to be modest. By not acknowledging compliments you're not only denying yourself a good feeling, but you're also denying the other person a good feeling. You are refusing his or her gift to you.

Notice the impact of your presence on your environment

and on the world. Observe how your actions influence other people's attitude, mood, and actions.

Look around. Notice how everyone seems to be in a big rush. Challenge yourself to take your time, to breathe, to take it all in. Be the person who makes the time for others—for example, be the person who lets others in front of you in a traffic jam. You'll see and feel a difference within you.

You might be asking yourself at this point, *Why would I do that? Why bother?* I say, do it because *you* are worth it. All these actions are gifts you give yourself, gifts that just happen to give to others too. It's a win-win situation. But keep in mind that this feels good only if you are genuine, only if you mean it—*not* if you're just doing it to look good.

Someone once told me that if you want to know who you are, look at your friends and the people you associate with. That's a good picture of who you are or who you will become. If the people who surround you reflect the positive image of who you are or of who you are striving to become, then *great.* But if they don't, it may be a good indication that you need to change your surroundings and find new friends.

True friends are people who encourage you to keep moving forward. They help when you need them, and they don't encourage you toward unhealthy habits or behaviors. Good friends offer support, not competition. If you have healthy friendships, embrace them by returning your kindness to these people. Friendship is truly a precious treasure.

Select your friends carefully, as they *do* reflect on you. I believe that if you surround yourself with millionaires, you will likely become one, and if you hang around with clowns, well, the next thing you know you're joining the circus. It may not be that drastic, but your surroundings do reflect on you and you in return reflect on them too. So choose your friends carefully.

If you say you are going to do something, *do it.* Give it your best—give it your true best—and always be kind. Do things in a loving manner. Learn from your mistakes, because when you blame someone for your mistakes, you are not learning. And you are mostly going to repeat that same mistake again. Accept your mistake and live your life. Everyone makes mistakes; it is part of learning.

Here is something really important: Being rude doesn't do anyone any good. It can potentially hurt someone and will hurt you in return. Your conscience will likely not let you off the hook easily; you might have a hard time falling asleep thinking of the way you handled yourself toward another person. So think twice before doing or saying things that could be hurtful. Ask yourself, *Is this really worth it?*

In trying to portray yourself as a successful person, it's important not to treat others as though they are inferior to you. Trust me, people see right through that, and it can backfire quickly. The effect may be the opposite of what you hoped—that is, people will likely see you as insecure rather than successful.

Remember

Remember the feeling you had as a kid, when the colors were so bright and Grandma's hugs were ever so reassuring. Remember how pure each feeling felt. Remember having a laugh that hurt so bad but you couldn't stop it. That is living life as it should be lived—to its fullest!

To know how good life is and how you should feel, think of your first bike and how happy you were to realize that you could ride it by yourself. This was likely the feeling of freedom—feeling the air on your face, seeing everything go by so fast, wanting to go faster and faster, wanting to feel that rush. Remember when you pedaled so fast you felt your legs couldn't keep up with the speed of the pedals. That, to me, is a feeling of pure joy—*joie de vivre*!

Try to find that feeling again. As adults, we often don't allow ourselves that feeling or stop it, as we either think it's not cool or we fear being seen and judged. You might think things like "I'm a grown-up and shouldn't act like this." Allow yourself to feel good, to feel free. To do that fully, you can't care about what you might think others may think or say about you.

Be happy in your own skin. Love who you are and don't compare yourself to others. Keep your friendships as alive and as pure as possible. Try to avoid competing with others, as it can corrupt your initial thoughts of them. Competition can easily become poisonous to a friendship.

Honesty—live it. Tell the truth, don't lie. I'm sure you have heard this many times. Really, if you say you're going to do something, then do it. If you have no intentions on following through with a promise, don't say it.

Say what you mean and do it. When you talk to people, don't make excuses like you're busy and you've got to go. Enjoy their conversation; look at their expressions and their smile. *Take* the time; *make* the time. In conversation, you will learn something in one way or another; it will make you feel great. You know it's true.

Whatever you do, don't set yourself up for failure. If you're witnessing someone making a mistake, help him or her. Don't just sit there and watch without warning him or her. Don't let little things bother you; life is too short to bother with them.

If you know something is not good for you from past experiences, deal with it. And don't do it again; learn from your last mistake. You know yourself so always be true to yourself. There's no need and really no point in lying so why do it? It won't prove anything anyway.

You know what is right and what is wrong. Follow what your heart tells you. If you really don't know, find out. And if you don't know where to find advice, ask someone you trust, someone who has your best interests in mind and wants what's best for you.

Relax. Go ahead, take a hot bath. Relax and enjoy the good things. Take time to enjoy your life. This moment, your moment, is *your* life, so it's in your best interest to treat yourself well. If you don't, who will?

When you do things, don't wait until the last minute to do it, because you will need to rush and may forget something. That will put more stress back on your shoulders. Try avoiding unnecessary stress and frustrations, which are often felt when you rush—rather, try doing things when they need to be done and doing them at your own pace.

When you do something that needs to be done but are not enjoying, try your best to make it more enjoyable. For example, when doing the dishes, try whistling or turn on some of your favorite tunes. First thing you know, you're done and weren't terribly annoyed with the task.

Take time to talk to people. If you are waiting in line, strike up a conversation with the person ahead of or behind you. Who knows, you might learn a thing or two—or even create a new friendship.

Breathe deeply—anywhere, everywhere. When you inhale deeply, notice all the good air and the good things you are taking in, and when you exhale, let all the bad out.

You are who you think you are and will likely become what you say you are. If you're constantly saying, "Oh, I'm such a loser," well, don't be surprised if one day you follow through. You're the only one who can set the bar for yourself so try setting it higher. Be good to yourself; thrive to aim higher, to improve yourself. I cannot emphasize this enough.

I grew up near Niagara Falls. My friend and I would ride our bikes to the falls as often as we could and enjoy the beautiful scenery. A few years passed, and I took my daughter to see the falls. We went on the *Maid of the Mist*, a tour boat that brings you close to the falls. Seeing my daughter's face covered with mist brought me real joy and made me think of when I was a kid and used to be covered with mist. That moment made me think how wonderful and beautiful my life was.

It is so nice when you can capture special moments like these. Life brings you a lot of special moments, and recognizing them makes them great, memorable moments. The feeling that comes with good memories is true a friend. That feeling is joy.

Take 6 care

Please, try to not to hold grudges or any negative feeling, as they're only bad for you, not for others. Why impose such a negative feeling on yourself? No one benefits from them. Try to set yourself up for success, not failure.

Negative feelings can keep from being creative. And negative feeling can be positive if you use them toward getting better. Learning from your mistakes is great, as long as you *do* learn. You will repeat the same mistakes if you do not learn from them the first time. So remember to be kind to yourself; why put more stress on yourself? A certain level of stress in life is okay, but adding unnecessary stress can be toxic and deteriorate your body.

Work out, exercise, try yoga, lift weights, jog a little, go for a walk. Do whatever you choose to do and do it for yourself, for your health.

Everyone exercises with different goals. Some want to have big muscles and some just want to be toned. As long as you exercise with a healthy heart while having fun, you exercise for *you* and for the good reasons of staying healthy and getting more energy. The more you move, the more energy you have. This seems strange, but it's just like the more you laugh and smile, the more likely you are to feel happy.

When you speak on the phone, try smiling. You'll likely notice that you are talking about positive things and less likely to complain. Try putting yourself in situations that will make you feel good, that will make you feel as if you're at your best.

Go window shopping and treat yourself. Just bring a smile to yourself, which will make your heart feel good again. See yourself smile again. Just remember, you always want to be in good situations. The more you smile, the more others who cross your path will feel like smiling as your happiness brings them a good feeling. Keep that feeling alive! If you don't have a smile on your face, figure out why that is and try to deal with that situation.

You likely *want* to smile because, let's face it, smiling makes you feel great and makes others feel pretty good too. Recognize that deep down you *want* to feel good, to be happy, and to have energy to do everything you want to do. When you do feel good, happy, and healthy, you can help others feel great in return.

LIFE IS GOOD when you smile. You have *joi de vivre.*

Get a coffee or whatever you enjoy. Visit with a friend. Sit down in front of a fountain. Look at your life in action and think, *Hey this is awesome. My life really rocks right now!*

Time can easily be taken for granted. Just remember that the only time you own is *right now*, so make the best of it.

Focus on the *right now.* Enjoy *the right now.* It is *right now* that you are reading this. *Now* prepares you for tomorrow.

Love your body. Look at your hands—at your fingers, your nails. Take the time to really look at your arms and remember the things you have lifted and carried with them. Be proud of your body. You are the one taking care of it, so feed it well and treat it with care and with great respect.

Feel good about your looks—not in a materialistic or vain way but as you truly are. Carry yourself in the way you want others to see you, the way you truly are. A lot of this lies in your attitude too. Try not to concentrate on your "flaws"; look at your assets instead. For example, if you think you have a "big butt" and keep emphasizing that, don't be surprised if others comment on it. Concentrate on your awesome hair, your flawless skin—or better yet, your incredible personality or your sense of humor—and that's what people will notice.

It is all in the way you look at things—at life. Your attitude can help determine how good your day will be.

If something bothers you *fix it*. Don't get in the habit of complaining about things that bother you. This isn't just a bad habit; it also is irritating to others who pick up a negative feeling, a negative energy, when around you. Doesn't that sound like something you would want to avoid?

This is why I emphasize keeping positive energy, having good manners, and being good to yourself and to others. It's like a big chain reaction of good feelings going around and coming right back.

Life is great.

Enjoy living it!

Your 7nergy

Go for a walk. It will clear your mind, and with a clear mind you have a better idea of what you want. When you know what you want, it gives you energy to accomplish what you need to do.

Living life to the best of your ability, doing the best that you can do in everything, and being kind to yourself is the best way to attain a fulfilled life.

Your heart is your energy, your soul, so be nice to yourself.

Smell the flowers. Look at healthy relationships and look at what you love. Feel your energy and share your energy. Really find out what your dream is. When you know it, just go for it—live it, make it happen. If you are living your dream, my friend, enjoy everything about it. Help others realize their dreams too. Don't waste your time with gossip and rumors; life is too short for things that can lead only to judging others (likely wrongfully).

Most of us know this stuff, but ...

- *Do you still have your manners?*
- *Are you living your dreams?*
- *Are you the best person you can be?*
- *Are you allowing others to judge you?*

- *Are you enjoying, embracing, **living** life?*
- *Be nice and feel it. Help someone have a nice day.*

Enjoy the food you eat. Use moderation when eating, as with everything in life. Go out for a nice supper to celebrate a special occasion. The bonding and the entertainment you have with others matters. Food seems to taste a lot better with great company. It can be a nice treat in itself, but the company of others that makes it real.

My mother told me that when she was a little girl, after the Second World War, most people didn't have much money. They didn't have a refrigerator; they had an icebox that would keep things cold for only a short period. My grandfather would go to the store and purchase one brick of ice cream, and then he would gather all the kids around the table. He would set that brick of ice cream on the table and slowly open all four sides flat on the table. Then he would take a knife and slowly cut the brick of ice cream into one-inch slices. All the children would have one tasty slice of ice cream on their own plate.

Now, that was a tasty treat. But it is the interaction and the bond that really made it a special moment. The ice cream alone was not the real treat; the treat was the bond and the stories that were told. At that moment, everyone felt special. Also that treat was rare. It wasn't often that they got ice cream, so when they did, it was very special.

Try new food. You may not like the taste of some of it, but you will likely discover a new taste that you really enjoy. Don't deprive yourself of foods you like but eat it in moderation. Like everything in life, try not to make things more complicated than they actually are.

Some diets can make eating complicated. They require

counting calories, measuring portions, ignoring your taste buds—avoiding fat or sodium or anything tasty. Don't complicate things. Just be good to yourself and try to eat food that it truly is *food*.

Try to have a healthy relationship with food—that is, don't try to make food something that isn't. Food can sometimes feel comforting but don't let it become your best friend. When you do that, it becomes hard to eat in moderation. Keep it simple: eat when you're hungry, stop when you're satisfied, and try burning off some of that energy with exercise.

If you start wondering if you're complicating things too much, remind yourself of our ancestors. Ask, "Was this something they did? Could they have survived without it?"

Always *relax* and be yourself. Take a deep breath and remember who you are. Every minute, every breath, is life—*your life.*

Breathe in life with every breath. Think positive thoughts and let only the positive enter your body, mind, and soul. Don't rush. If you have somewhere to go, leave ahead of time and arrive prepared and in a good mood.

On a nice walk in nature, ask yourself, *What do I see, hear, and smell?* The beautiful trees, the leaves on the ground, the sound they make when you walk on them, the fresh air, the little breeze.

I love the mountains, and walking in the woods always makes me feel great. I hear the water from the creek; I hear the birds signing; I breathe the great mountain air. I sit down on a log and have a sip of water and just enjoy nature. This is a way for me to get peace from the everyday noise, which I tend to get used to. That makes me happy.

Find little joys in life and make those feelings last. Enjoy something as simple as the first, perfectly brewed cup of coffee you have in the morning. Make that little feeling of joy last all morning. Allow yourself to feel the happiness inside. Don't tell yourself it's silly or pathetic to think that such a minor detail can make you happy. Instead, feed that feeling; make it grow. It's really not about the coffee; it's about the spark of joy you got from it. That little spark can work wonders if you keep it lit. It will likely make you feel like smiling more, laughing more, wishing others a good day.

And first thing you know, you're having a pretty positive day. The more you smile, the more others who cross your path will feel like smiling as your happiness brings them a good feeling. Keep that feeling alive. If you don't have a smile on your face, figure out why that is and try to deal with that situation.

Enjoy the life you're living. If it's not what you want to be doing and you don't like your surroundings or the attitude you have, change it.

Be *true* to yourself. Know what you like and don't like and try to surround yourself with people, activities, and pastimes that increase your feeling of happiness.

Try to always put yourself in a situation and position that you want to be in. Don't let yourself get in a position you don't want to be, in and if you feel like you are stuck in a negative or unhealthy situation, try to get out of it in good manners and with self-respect.

You're bored? Color in a coloring book; doodle like you used to when you were a kid. When was the last time you drew a picture just for the fun of it? Try it. It's amazing how liberating drawing, coloring, or painting can be. Let yourself enjoy this.

Laugh as much as possible but avoid laughing at others or their misfortunes. If you have done something silly, allow yourself to laugh about it. It's okay—if it's funny, laugh.

Are you happy to be you? If not, figure out what the problem is. Life is when you feel it in your heart. Be yourself. Nobody can be yourself but you. Remember to live that thing called life.

Sometimes happiness can be achieved by letting go. The past is gone. Sure, you have memories and should keep good memories alive, but try not to dwell on past issues. Try to learn from your mistakes and move on. Try to avoid repeating the same mistakes. Avoid feeding negative memories of the past; these can haunt you and are pretty much useless to you now. If something from your past bothers you, take a good look at it, confront it, accept that it happened and that it cannot be changed, make peace with it in your heart and move on. Allow yourself to be *happy*.

Respect

Respect is one of the best words and one of the best feelings. That's because you need respect to love.

Think hard about this: do you really respect yourself?

Do you see yourself as a good person?

Do you think you are better than anyone?

To respect others, don't think that you are better than anyone else. We're all in the same boat here. But most people lack respect for others. They don't care about other's belongings or about other's feelings.

Respect for others will take you far in life. Again, treat yourself with respect; do everything with dignity; walk tall and feel proud of yourself. Life is beautiful when everyone helps one another. Do things to your best ability and with good intentions.

If you want to be nice to someone do it.

If you want to be rude or mean to someone don't.

One day, as I was casually coming out of a building, I opened the door to let a couple of women in. It looked like it may have been a mother and daughter, and the older woman was using a walker. They both walked forward and thanked me. The older woman looked straight into my eyes as she was slowly walk and again said thank you. I said, "It's my pleasure. Have a good day."

She said, "You just made it good."

Those words alone made me feel so good (I guess I really needed to hear them); they gave me so much energy that I could have opened the door for everyone all day. I could not believe that I could get so much energy with such a small comment from such a tiny lady.

When you feel positive energy like that, try to make it last all day. Feed that energy and don't hold back. Let that feeling bloom inside you; don't be shy about it. Let it make you smile. Enjoy it Savor it.

Try to avoid saying "sorry" all the time. That can easily become a habit. Apologize only when you have something to apologize about. And when you do apologize, be genuine about it. Be truly intent on not repeating the error for which you need to apologize.

In a drive-thru line one day, I decided that I would cover the changes for the person in the vehicle behind me. When I did this, it felt great. It felt right. I decided to drive away before the person could acknowledge my gesture, as I wanted to remain anonymous. It didn't cost me very much, but it was one of the greatest feelings. It made me smile.

It's often little gestures like these that can really make a difference and give you that *joie de vivre* feeling. So have a good day every day. Knowing that you've made someone's day better really feels great.

It's my understanding that most (if not all) people want to eat well, drink well, be healthy, look good, feel good, go on nice vacations, drive a nice reliable vehicle, own a beautiful home, and build up a nice bank account. It's great to want to achieve goals toward self-improvement, but as we look ahead, we can sometimes forget to look at all the great things we have in the present, right in front of us. Once in a while, look around, notice how good you have it and be thankful.

It's easy to get in a habit of complaining about the things that aren't as great as you would like them to be. It's a good idea to remember that complaining about little things can block you from living a happy life. When you get in the habit of noticing the nice things, your life feels great. You see positive things all around you and after a while don't notice negativity as much.

I don't mean to say you should live in denial or be oblivious to what's going on in your surroundings. I simply mean that there are positive ways of interpreting things, even in what may appear to be a negative situation. It's just a matter of taking the time to notice them and be thankful for them. A lot of how we perceive our lives lies in our attitude—the mindset we have toward life and toward everything in our surroundings.

Always remain calm or at least try to. There is no need for going haywire, no need to get upset. Getting stressed out doesn't do anyone any good. Just keep your composure.

Life might sometimes be hard but don't get discouraged. Things always seem to fall into place some way, somehow. See challenges that present themselves as great opportunities for you to stand up and show the world what you're made of. Confront your issues, face your challenges, and move on. Try not to look back and dwell on these issues. If they have been resolved, allow yourself to move forward. Grab ahold on life and *live* it.

Live free. You have only one life to live so live it. Live it well.

Every morning, say thank you. "Today is a brand-new day. Thank you."

Be kind but no a pushover. Don't let others take advantage of you and try not to let insults get to you. You know who you are. Try to be strong and confident in your thoughts and in your mind. Respect and love yourself. When you do, it's much easier for others to treat you as you should be treated.

If you want to know who you are, look at the people you choose to interact with. What kind of people do you associate with? Don't try to be something or someone you're not, because that can only last for so long, and in the meantime you can get confused as to who you really are. Be true to yourself and to your values. Try not to lie to yourself, pretending you are something other than what you are.

When you do things for someone, do it with dignity and respect, do not do things self-indulgently. Be proud but don't brag.

When you do things, make sure you do it to the best of your ability—do it so well that you would be proud of putting your signature on it. Once you've accomplished something that you would be proud to stamp your name on, that's when you know you have given it your very best.

When you start something, finish it.

Love your life and
live it well

Have control so you don't judge. Know who you are. No one is entitled to have power over you. Live free of fear.

I'm happy and not afraid to show it but don't judge me for it. When I smile, laugh out loud, praise others, or express my love to others, don't judge me. Don't judge me without taking the time to know me.

A lot of how you perceive your life lies in your attitude—the mindset you have toward life and everything in your surroundings.

If you look good, people will say you look good, and that makes you feel good. Looking good is a reflection of how you feel. Behaving well is a reflection of who you are. Have class and be an altogether classy person.

No one likes to be judged; everyone likes compliments. The only one who has the power to judge you is you so go easy on yourself. If you want to be good, you likely will be good. The first thing people see is others' appearance, and it is hard not to judge at first sight.

Everyone has his or her own beliefs and stereotypes. Always treat yourself with the utmost respect. That way, people will respect you. When you are respected, you are more likely to be respectful to others.

You have a dream so go for it. Don't let others decide this for you. If it feels right in your heart, pursue your dream. You're the one who's going to miss out if you don't. Help, don't judge. Smile, be happy, and help others.

If you want a good life, be good. If you want what's best, be the best. Your actions are really a reflection of you.

Live well. Live this life to your fullest. You have only one chance to live. Remember, this is a one-time-only offer. You're only on this beautiful planet *once.* Make it count. A lot of your perception of life lies in your *attitude.* Your life is good; try to see how good it is. I'm alive and my world is great. Thank you!

There's only one chance to prove you are good so live life well. Don't take life for granted.

Maybe you're reading this book on the beach or in the mountains or during a camping trip or while soaking in the tub or in your bed. Wherever you may be, put the book down for a minute, look around, and notice how beautiful your surroundings are, how beautiful life is, and how beautiful nature is. Close your eyes and take it in.

Life is too beautiful not to notice all its greatness. Be thankful for it all. Say thank you for the beautiful sunset and the sound of birds first thing in the morning. The list of things to be thankful for can go forever.

I am living in heaven, a heaven on earth. Love is in my

heart. Don't lose yourself; keep your heart youthful. Be joyful, be happy, and enjoy who you are.

If you are a working man or woman, be very thankful for your job. It is something that you do most of the time, so make sure that your environment is pleasing to you. Try to be pleasant around others, as it will help make their lives more pleasant. Try to make people laugh. It doesn't matter what the situation is, make the most of it. Make the most of life and enjoy it.

Treat everyone with respect. At the end of the day, we are all humans. Let's just love one and other. There is lots of love in your heart to share. And tomorrow morning you will have even more in your heart, because you're allowing it to grow.

It doesn't matter where you live or where you sleep at night. I have slept in trenches that I dug myself, and I have slept in fine hotels. It didn't seem to matter much where I slept, because at the end of the day, when I closed my eyes, I always knew who I was. I know that I can go to sleep with a clear conscience, saying, "I have done my best and tomorrow I will do even better."

I live my life well by appreciating all the little things: the sound of high heels on concrete, the crunching leaves, the waves of the ocean surf, and the smell of a fresh cup of coffee, a summer barbeque, a fresh cut flower, and a recently picked green apple.

I appreciate my life. I appreciate being human.

Helping people helps your heart grow bigger.

Everyone wants to be good and to do good. If others live their dream, it feels good to them. Don't for a moment feel sad or jealous, and do not judge them. Help them to the best of your ability and knowledge.

Most people are nice and do want what is best for you. If you visit their home, town, city, or park, they want you to enjoy yourself. If you go to a restaurant or are invited to home, people there want you to enjoy yourself. So the best thing to do is thank them genuinely.

Help, don't judge. Smile, be happy, and help others.

Don't judge. It does nothing for you or for your ego. Judging communicates a lack of love and respect. When I say, "Don't judge me," it doesn't mean I have done wrong and am trying to hide it. I simply mean, "Don't stand in my way of loving life and living it fully."

When you want to live—to live free and to live your dream—do it with respect. Respect yourself; respect your likes and dislikes; respect your dreams.

If people are not like you or do not look like you or are not as rich as you or as good looking as you, don't judge them for their appearance. Do strike up a conversation if they really want to talk with you. Then, my friend, welcome them into your world. Be happy.

Try your best to always (or as much as possible) feel happy. Why not?

Find little joys in life and make those feelings last. You just found the best parking spot, and it made your day. Allow yourself to feel the happiness inside. Don't tell yourself that it's silly or pathetic to think that such a minor detail can make you happy. Instead, feed that feeling; make it grow. It's really not about the coffee or the parking spot; it's about the spark of joy you got from it.

That little spark can work wonders if you keep it lit up. It will likely make you feel like smiling more, laughing more, and wishing others a good day. And first thing you know, you're having a pretty positive day. The more you smile, the more others who cross your path will feel like smiling, as your happiness brings them a good feeling. Keep that feeling alive.

Remember to treat others the way you would like to be treated.

Be someone that you can count on. Be someone that other people can count on and be trusted. Mean what you say and say what you mean—politely!

Living life to the best of your ability, doing the best that you can do in everything, and being kind to yourself is the best way to attain a fulfilled life.

That is life when you feel it in your heart. Be yourself, nobody can be yourself but you.

Remember to live that thing called life.

Be proud 10 of yourself

Think of what you want and go for it. That is probably the best advice you can tell someone.

Laughing is good but not when it's behind someone's back. If the person you are talking about is not with you, talking about him or her does nothing for you and does even less for that person.

What goes around comes around. This if often called karma, which is the circle of cause and effect of your deeds. It is the reactions to your actions. It is getting what you deserve (good or bad). If karma doesn't find you, I guarantee you that your conscience will not let you off the hook easily!

There is no need to stick your nose in someone else's business. It is not up to you to tell others what to do. You can assist them and guide them toward what you think is the right path, but don't allow yourself to mind other people's business—you are not entitled to it.

Watch out for your ego. Don't just focus on yourself; avoid being egotistical. Try building you self-confidence instead. (Ego and self-confidence are two very different things.)

Life consists of many tests. How well you do in these tests lies in the way you have managed to deal with them.

It is your life to live, not for others to live for you. Live your dream. Don't judge other people's dreams, and don't let anyone judge yours.

Fill your life with all the goodness that comes your way and with all the laughter that you can handle. Laugh as much as you can. Surround yourself with very pleasant environments. Live your dream. Treasure your life—your everything.

Don't be scared of running out of dreams. More dreams will come your way so live them to the fullest. Dream lots; dream *big*. Don't waste your time with people who say that your dreams are too big. My theory is that dreams are meant to be whatever size you make them, and there should never be a limit in their size.

Living life is fun and everyone should enjoy it.

Whatever children do, they live life with love and harmony and without judgment. Take a look at a drawing by a child. Notice that it is the child's true expression. Listen to how children's laughter seems to come straight from the heart. Remember when you were a child. You had no worries, no peer pressure. You just did the things that you loved with harmony, without judgment—pure Joi de vivre.

You have 100 percent pure energy; you want to live life. Try living in a good, respectful way, without hurting your fellow brothers and sisters. Try not to judge. Ask yourself if you are entitled to do so—"Who am I to judge?"

It's all about you. Your life is about you. When others come into your life, it is up to you whether to have a friendship with them or not. When people ask for help, take a look at your attitude; do you choose to help guide them, smile, give them love, appreciate their life, make them feel love when they're around you. Or do you turn away from them?

This is my first time living on this planet (that I can remember). Like everyone else, I want the best of what's out there; I want what is best for my family, my friends, and everyone in my life. I want a good life—and I do have a good life.

Do what you really want to do in life; you are the only one who knows the real you. If you are not sure who you really are, ask God—the one who is watching over you—for the answer, and you will know.

You can always learn from others; you just need to open your mind to it.

The best feeling is to be proud of yourself. Tell yourself that you are proud of yourself and of tell others you are proud of them.

To be confident, live with the self-image that you want. Live with no fear and enjoy every moment of your life. Live each day with your true passion and purpose. Respect your abilities and feel that desire to live your dreams. You *can* feel it.

Do something that
will make you happy

Have an opened mind to everything that is happening. If you were to choose between good and bad, which would you choose? Well, then choose to be who you want to be. Choose right over wrong, choose healthy over lazy, choose love over hate, and live your life, my friend.

There is no need to lie. No need to think that you are better than others. No need to judge. But be proud of the good person that you are, the awesome person you have become.

Joie de vivre is living happily and lively, living free, feeling good and feeling real. As you live this way, you can accomplish anything. Any goal you set for yourself is achievable, or else the thought of it wouldn't have entered your mind. In other words, if the thought came to your mind, it is because your mind thinks it can be done. What's getting in the way of accomplishing this goal? Think hard, because I can almost guarantee that there is only one standing in your way, preventing you from doing this: *you*

This is my life. I will live my life the best way that I can.

When you play a sport, do it for fun or to meet people or for the exercise or to keep fit or to maintain good health. Of course, everyone wants to win. Winning is fun and the feeling of winning is great. If you're playing with your friends and are having fun, laughing out loud, breathing the fresh air, and giving it your all, you have won. You are surrounded by loved ones and are having a blast. That's *really* what the game is about (not so much about points and stuff).

Try to be a good sport. If your team didn't get the most points, be a good sport about it and give credit where credit is due. Congratulate the other team and keep having fun. If your team got the most points, be gracious about it and don't gloat—no one likes a showoff. There's nothing wrong with having a little competition during sporting events or while playing a game with friends, but try to keep it at a fun level. And avoid judgment; that level of competition really doesn't look good on anyone.

You do need time for you. In the morning, take your cup of coffee (that is, if you drink coffee) and enjoy that moment. No need to take all day, but take some time for yourself to relax and sort out you thoughts, and then go on with you day with a clear mind.

A night I as I sit at my deck, I enjoy the beautiful day I had, and I look at what my life, at the things I had accomplished, at the dreams I am so excited to live. In the middle of the night, as I look at the stars, I try to look beyond the stars. During those times I ask myself, *Is everything in my life the way I want it? Am I the person I want to be ?* I just want to be happy and share my happiness with someone.

I just want to be myself.

I know from the deepest part of me that I want to be happy. I want to be the best that I want to be. I want to have the best in life. I know that *everyone* wants the best in life. Most of us will do almost anything and everything to get it. That is the part where it is scary.

So, who set the bar? This fast-paced standard of living? Who is the one to whom you say, "I need this and I need that"? With all due respect and with all honesty, it is you. All of it is you. It is up to the individual to know what is important.

About criticism: Between you and me, most people are so afraid of criticism, they don't know how to take it. People have forgotten how to criticize nicely and that criticism can be good. Now we always take it like it's a bad thing.

Here I am, going as fast as possible to reach dead ends. Every person is rushing to buy the best Christmas gifts, to buy the biggest and the latest. Who are we all in a race with? Who is the winner? Is there a winner at all? Why is looking good in front of people so fucking important? Why is there a race? Did we all start that way?

We are chasing our own tales here. We can't wait to get a coffee, and we have a problem waiting two or three minutes in line for it so we can sit down and relax. When we do have our caffeinated and very tasty beverage, we plan our day, and we are soon off again. We don't have time to get supper; we get it delivered or stop in a drive-thru. We enjoy a family reunion, what, once a year at Thanksgiving? It should be more often than that, wouldn't you think?

This fast-paced lifestyle keeps us from being independent. Where is our quality of life? We all want it. We want the perfect mate, the perfect relationship, but we don't take time to look. We are too shit scared of wasting time.

It's time to take a deep breath and start to live and to pay attention to life—your life.

Always be 12 thankful

Acknowledge people with sincerity. Go ahead, shake a hand, hug a friend, or wave to someone. Look into people's eyes when you talk to them. People love to be acknowledged and appreciated.

Be generous with your smiles—trust me, you won't run out. Don't forget to smile at yourself when you see your reflection in the mirror; make it a habit. Smile at yourself after shaving or putting on makeup first thing in the morning. When you speak on the phone, put a smile on your face; the other person will feel happiness in your voice. Also do this on your voicemail greeting. It's hard to describe, but your tone really makes a difference. With a smile, you can significantly help improve someone's day.

Always listen, because others do have lots to say. Try to avoid interrupting, as it can quickly become a nasty habit.

Be diplomatic and nice; there's no need to ever be rude.

Be as grateful as possible for every minute of the day and for everything that is happening. It is happening because you let it.

Of course, be open minded. You might learn a thing or two.

Forgive others. You have to find it in your heart to really forgive. It is indeed through the act of forgiving someone that you can move forward in life. Forgiving and forgetting is hard to do sometimes. When you forgive others, you are not only helping them feel better, you are freeing yourself of lingering negative thoughts and feelings. When you truly forgive another person, you will feel as though a big weight has been lifted off your shoulders. Try doing this more often; you deserve it.

Show someone that they are good, that they mean something to you and have impacted your life. When you see or observe others doing something nice or just being good, tell them how nice that was of them, so they know that what they have done hasn't gone unnoticed. I received some mail from my boss some time ago, and my first thought was, "Oh, here we go. Now what?" So I opened the envelope and it held a birthday card. I was amazed at how much energy that card gave me; it totally made my day. When you think, *Why bother giving a card?* (or whatever it is you're planning on doing for someone), remind yourself of a little gesture that that has made a big difference for you, something that made you feel special. Kind little gestures *do* matter, and they *do* make a difference. *Do not* underestimate the power of kindness.

Contribute toward making someone feel happy, or happier. I think that is one of the highlights that makes life so great. Go ahead, buy someone a cup of coffee, give someone a flower, help friends move, help a neighbor shovel her sidewalk. These kind gestures will make you feel great for a long time and will likely be remembered by the person you're helping. Don't do it for the reward; do it for joie de vivre.

Allow yourself to learn from others.

Tell people that you love them—don't be shy! When you feel it, show it. Tell your significant other that you love him or her—and do it often. Listen to others and provide them with support, comfort, and *respect*. If that's something you consider ridiculous, well, don't expect to get it from others. I repeat: what goes around comes around. If you want respect, love, comfort, and all that good stuff, you have to offer it.

Avoid double standards. Generally, people want equality, and when things aren't fair, they notice it pretty quickly and often become angry. This can lead to negative feelings. So try to avoid being the source of double standards.

If you are at fault or have done something wrong, own up to it; admit what you have done and move on. Live life.

Surround yourself with people who you enjoy being around and who make you enjoy who you are when you are with them. That is a good way to live. Do not ever let negative people influence you. Trust me, it is not worth it. Try to surround yourself with positive people, and make people feel good just being around you.

Tell people that you appreciate them and their good actions. Also create or maintain eye contact with people. Only an honest, self-confident person can look into another person's eyes. This is a message others can read (likely subconsciously), so allow yourself to be read this way. Find the confidence to do this, and others will have more confidence in what you are saying. When thanking someone, do it with eye contact. Say "I love you" while looking straight into the other person's eyes. That's when your words can be felt, and it's a pretty strong feeling.

It is not always an actions that matters, but the feeling you (or others) get from that action. Think of a great book you read or an awesome movie you saw; it's not really what happened in these stories that made them so good, but the feeling you got from them.

Enjoy all of your actions and make sure they are what you truly want.

Be thankful for all the good things that are happening in your life: your health, your wealth, your happiness, the love that you share, and all the things that nature has given you.

Here are some good questions you can ask to get to know yourself better and to understand more of what you really want. When you do understand what you want, your life will become exceptionally amazing.

- Do you live a really good life? Is this the life you really want?
- Do you know what love is? Do you know who and what you love?
- Do you love? Do you love the things that you do and the people you associate with?
- Do you know who you love? Is the person in your life really the person you want to be with? Do you click? Do you have a good connection? Do you respect that person and does that person respect you?

Because love is the best feeling, surround yourself with many things you love and with the people you love most.

Nothing can go wrong when you are surrounded with love. That's a good feeling, right?

Knowledge is powerful, but only if you put it into practice. To put it into practice, take this book with you and to read every chance you have—when you are waiting in line or on the bus, or waiting for a friend for coffee. Read it again and again. The fun part is that, when you read, you will think of something that you didn't think the first time you read it. It is not exactly about what you are reading; it is what you think and the feelings that you have while reading.

Take time to make each moment count. When you touch someone, such as when you shake someone's hand, realize that was a good handshake. Be aware that one person smelled like gum and another like flowers. Feel the moment and enjoy it. If it's bad, let it go.

I think of the following saying a lot, because I think it's so true: "It's not how many times you fall that matter; it's how many times you get up." Make the positive outcomes count, and try not to look at the obstacles. If you need to look back, make it a learning experience; learn from your mistakes but don't dwell on them.

You must want real life—not fake or filler—so go ahead and live the real life that you wish for. Again, you are the only one in control of that. Are you going to allow it or stop it?

People choose their lifestyle. Be honest with yourself and choose the lifestyle you want. All good things will come to you. Remember, all things that you want are possible for you to have.

Ladies and gentlemen, be kind. Whether you are rich or poor behave with proper manners. Be proud of yourself, walk proud, stand tall, and just be you. Be proud to be you.

No one else can be you—just you. So represent yourself in the best way you can; no one else can do this for you.

When you go to sleep, do it in a thankful and confident frame of mind, and all will be well.

To live a magnificent life, surround yourself with the best and become the best. But first you have to be able to recognize what "the best" is. First, you have to know what you want. To recognize what truly makes you joyful, find out what you love. Is it painting? Running? Working out? Spending time with friends? Swimming? Working? It is a waste of your time and efforts to surround yourself with things you don't care about. Second, you always have to be noble and truly honest with yourself. What you need and want will be there for you, but you need to acknowledge what you need. That is what makes your heart sing.

I work away from home. When my daughter, Dominique, was little, I would bring her a little something. Her mom would tell her that Daddy was coming today. And Dominique would make something to give me when I arrived. One time she drew a nice castle and wrote, "To: Dad From: Dominique." The way she gave me her present meant a lot, because she put a lot of effort into it and thought of her dad coming home the whole time she was coloring. And she didn't even color outside the lines. The thought of her thinking of me is what made it such a special gift. I got a tattoo of that castle to remind me of my daughter.

Dare to be

Your thinking creates your life, and with your actions you're living it. Think of who you are and become what you want to be.

The formula to living a great life is believing in yourself. When you believe in yourself, the sky's the limit. You can walk taller and you can live with yourself as someone you can trust. Be who you want to be; yes, be true to you. Love yourself so you can love others; respect yourself so you can respect others. When you accept yourself and you are happy and you love yourself, go ahead and love others. Make the most of yourself. Do the best you can do and mind your own business.

Have faith in your thoughts. Our constant thoughts make us what we are. That's why it is so important to surround yourself with what you want and to speak of what you want to be. You are good and always will be.

My mother told me once about the door knob test. If you are going in a room for a meeting or speech but you do not feel good about it, don't open that door. Walk around and ask yourself why you have to be in that room. When you realize why and you have a positive feeling, open that door.

Remember that wealth and opportunities will come. And that life is very generous; life will give you the happiness, the wealth, the health, the love that you deserve. Pay attention to your life.

Here's a little quote from, Mark Twain:

Twenty years from now you will be more disappointed by the things you didn't do than by the ones you did do. So throw off the bowlines. Sail away from the safe harbor. Catch the winds in your sails. Dream. Discover.

Have faith in yourself. Always believe in yourself. Dreams do come true so be true to your dreams and be true to you. Do *not* let fear be in your way *ever*. Most of your fears have been created by you, so you can get rid of them. If you have the power to create your fears, you also have the power to face them and eliminate them. When you have a dream and you truly want it, don't let fear get in the way. Be calm, trust, and have faith. You are living *now*. Are you doing what you want to do? If so, good. Life is great. If not, what is stopping you?

Don't spend time arguing or listening to people complaining. You have much better things to do. Ask yourself, *Do I really want to absorb this negativity into my mind?*

Instead of raising your voice when you want to make a point or while in an argument, try to keep your composure and try not to yell. People you are addressing will listen to you so much more if you are calm. Not only will you be able to get your point across, but you also won't lose face or credibility if you remain calm. Trust me; it works.

So speak up with good intentions. Use your voice if you want to be heard. But there is no need to yell or be bossy.

Believe that what you have to say is important; give credit to your thoughts. There is nothing to be afraid of.

Joie de vivre, the joy of living, comes when you are true to yourself, when you are as close as possible to who you truly are. Ask yourself what you really want to do, how to be better, and how to really be *you*. Ask yourself who you really are and how to be the best that you can be. Listen, because when you listen, you will know.

Be as close as possible to your true self. That is when you are at peace with yourself.

Enjoy the right now. Focus on the now. It makes a happier tomorrow and makes yesterday better. Live life. You are stronger than you think. Keep living to the best of your abilities. Be someone that you can count on, someone that people can have faith in.

Think of what you want instead of what you don't want. If you want money, talk to people who have it.

Remember to love yourself and respect yourself, so you can respect and love others. Do what makes you feel good. I want to feel good and I want everyone to be happy—truly happy, wealthy, healthy, and loved.

Watch out what you wish for, because you will get it. You will get everything that you think the most of—good or bad. You will attract what you nourish in your mind, what you speak about, and what you act toward.

Most people want to live well and do well. People tend to forget, and it's good to be reminded. And discover something new. Follow your heart and be kind and generous. Love your surroundings, love yourself, and love everyone. Listen to what your heart is telling you. Have faith. Learn to trust your heart.

Close your eyes. How do you see yourself? There is no

competition. It's entirely you with yourself. Write down what you want and how you plan to achieve it. It is all going to happen if you believe what you want out of life. Self-confidence is a must. Believe in yourself and remember to breathe in the air in your surroundings.

Your actions are a reflection of you. Take a look at your actions, because they can give you an idea as to who you truly are. If you do good actions with good intentions, that is good. But if you keep doing wrong or bad actions or even actions with bad intentions, you likely need to reflect on this.

Remember that life is what you make it. Have a good attitude; always take in the positive and the *love*. If you have a good, loving, and positive attitude, it makes you strong enough to overcome whatever is thrown at you. You get in life what you have put in. C'est si bon! (It's so good!)

When you were born, you were the closest to the *real you*. When you were young, you were so innocent and so free and so true to yourself. As you grew, you forget who you were. Stay calm, listen to your heart, and you will know exactly who you really are. Please take the time to listen to *you*.

If you are a man, be a gentleman. If you are a woman, be a lady. Be there if someone needs you. Truly be there. Take time to be the shoulder people can cry on.

Life becomes amazing

Life is all about learning. Don't forget to make time for learning. Life is definitely not a race to get to the end as fast as possible. It is a journey. And it is being able to enjoy the every moment.

Everyone wins and win big, especially you, because you made friends. Play with noble actions that will make you proud of yourself. Love everyone. That's it. It is simple and it has been said over and over. The thing is, everyone knows the good stuff but doesn't put it into practice. Most people like to do what pleases them first and take the easy way. Remember, what you think about is what you put into practice. As the old saying goes, "Practice what you preach."

Love everything you do. Love your life. Live your life surrounded with *love*. Above all, love yourself.

If you want something in life, just think of it until you get it. When you do get it, be thankful for it, nurture it, maintain it, protect it, and keep desiring it.

Life becomes amazing when you fill it with love. It's all

about your attitude. You need to have faith. With faith, you will never live in fear. Just have faith. **Believe.**

Gatherings like anniversaries, holidays, and birthdays, are meant to be joyful; they are meant be a time to share happiness and to tell friends and family that you love and appreciate them. You are really happy when you share a meal with those you love and are a part of their lives. Treat every gathering like it's Thanksgiving, because a happy and healthy life is to be surrounded by those you love and to be thankful for their presence in your life.

Love your family. Let your heart grow. Share your heart. Your actions have to be good. Surround yourself with a positive and loving environment.

Help those who want help, who want to improve. Don't waste much of your time on those who don't. They are likely not ready, and your words may be perceived as criticism. By trying to help, you may in fact hurt them.

Use words of encouragement and praises other. Tell them that they can do it and they will.

Reaching success is exactly like riding a bike: you don't want to have to stop or to fall because a stick gets caught in your wheels. That stick is negativity, so take it out of your wheel, brush the dirt off your knees, get back on the bike and ride again without fear. You can ride without fear because your fall has made you wiser; you have learned to stay away from sticks, and you now know how to handle a fall.

When you think you can, you can. If you think you can't, my friend, you can't and you won't.

If you say you will do something, make sure that you do it. Make sure people can trust you by following through with your promise by doing what you say you will do. People respect loyalty and honesty.

Try not to get caught up in rumors and gossip. This will lead you nowhere When you speak, speak the truth. In the heat of a battle, keep your composure. Always!

If you want to do something, do it now. Don't wait until tomorrow, because tomorrow turns into a week, then a month, and then years. Just do it; make it happen.

The way you look at life is all in your attitude your perception, your thoughts, your beliefs. To increase your confidence and to maintain a positive attitude, take a look at my mom's recipe:

- 2 cups of love
- I teaspoon of happiness
- I teaspoon of well-being
- Mix all together and enjoy a nice cup of joie de vivre.

Have courage and know that your life is great and all is good.

Your outside appearance is a reflection of how you feel inside. Actions are louder and weigh more than words. It's the little everyday things that you do that count. Be in touch with your inner-self. Keep your dignity.

Feel your power that is inside you. Remember, walk with a full-of-life attitude. Be on your best behavior and be proud to be who you are. It is ultimately up to you to be the best that you can be.

We tend to complicate things for no reason at all. When we keep things less complicated, we can enjoy more of the things that really matter—our amazing life! We learn to smile again, to play again, to breathe in life, and to have fun. So get ahold on your life. Want it. You are worth it and deserve it. Smile to yourself. Find the joie de vivre—the joy of living.

Believe in your dreams and believe in yourself. Be thankful of all the little things that happen to you. Have such an impact that people feel good being around you. Say thank you for everything around you. Be yourself—your true self. Feel good by being you.

You have to know who you are and to not let insults bother you. Don't stick around where there's negativity. When people tell you something, look at their surroundings and look at the source. If their lifestyle is negative, drop what they told you.

Enjoy every single moment as the best as you can. Treat every moment like apple pie: enjoy the smell, appreciate the work that went into it, taste the crust and the cinnamon, and savor the chunks of apple.

Make your inner child live again. Share your smile. It's okay to laugh, and when you make others laugh, that will make you feel great. That moment is a good part of life. Cherish it. Be sure that at the end of every day you are proud of yourself; that you can go to sleep in peace, knowing that you helped someone; that you were there for that person that needed help; that you made someone's day; and that all the people you met are better because of your actions.

Life becomes amazing when you realize all the things that you have done, how much you have, and what you are going to accomplish.

I always strike up a conversation when it feels right. One day I said hi to a man and wished him a very nice day. He asked if I had served in the army, which I had. Then he told me that he was also in the army back in the day. He was supposed to fly in Normandy. A few nights before the flight, he and his colleagues got into a little bit of trouble, so he missed the flight. Two days later he went to Normandy. The few fellows that he knew before the flight and got into some trouble over did not make it. He told me, "When it's not your time, it's not your time."

He also told me that he was on a patrol to scout a particular area. They found the enemy they were looking for, but they were traveling into their direction. They couldn't hide, so they dug a small shale crape to lie in; it was the only cover or hiding they had. This ninety-two-year old man told me that he was scared, and he either passed out or went to sleep. What woke him up was the track of the tank rolling over him, but he stayed very quiet. After the tank was gone he stood up and was a bit hurt, but not badly. Again he said to me, "When it's not your time, it's not your time."

As I listened to his story, I felt the emotion that he must have felt, which made me realize how precious and how extraordinary our lives are. And he felt good being able to share his story. We both felt good. We were keeping eye contact, and we both understood the feeling behind his story.

By looking in his eyes while he was telling the story, I felt it. It made me realize how important life is and how much we do value our lives. Sometime it takes bigger lessons to realize it.

Be true to yourself. Know what you like and don't like and try to surround yourself with people, activities, and pastimes that increase your feeling of happiness.

The Lady and the Gentleman

Think of what you want, then go for it. It's all about having a healthy attitude.

If you are a woman, be a lady; if you are a man, be a gentleman. You are not just a woman in a fancy dress or a man in a suit; you are a person that understands your surroundings and respects others. Everyone wants to go from A to B, but it is how you get there that makes it true to you.

You are a strong person; with your body, your mind, and your emotions you make your presence count. People would like the good life, but only the ones who truly want it will get it. They become what they want to be and are proud to be who they are.

The confident ones are those who know who they are. They are comfortable with themselves and accept who they are with love.

Listen to what people have to say. To become someone special or to have an impact in someone's life, you have to care about others' needs and be there to help them in a respectful manner, to give them what they need with the attitude of a lady or a gentleman—with a smile and respect.

So, my friend, how do you want to live? People who love their life live it to the best of their ability. Always acts in a respectful manner, simply because you respect your surroundings. Be grateful for all situations that you encounter. Handle yourself with great pride and a good demeanor.

Enjoy your drink or coffee with others as you seize the moment. Enjoy people's company as they share their feelings and ideas with you. Don't interrupt, and give advice only if they want it or need it.

The woman and the man that I am describing are calm because they took the time to look ahead and observe all possibilities so they do not feel rushed or stressed.

If take healthy actions, you will be healthy. Good behavior, good motives, and right actions every day are what count. You do well because you want to do well.

The woman and man who are gentle are kind to themselves and to everyone. The lady and gentleman always deliver kind gestures, because they care. They care about their environment and the people they interact with; they know that their actions will affect them.

Love your life and respects others. It is easy to care when the feeling is present. Always be yourself and live by how you see yourself.

You want to have the lady's or the gentleman's touch. Ladies and gentlemen are strong. Strong people do no harm for selfish satisfaction and can admit when they are in the wrong. They can be strong when things are not going well; they can be caring on a raining day.

Smell the flowers, look at healthy relationships, and look at what you love.

Love and respect
your parents

The lady who loves her mother knows she can always count on her mom for advice on the most important things in life that she should know. She receives her mother's love, which is the most comforting love. With this love and affection, the woman became who she is today.

A gentleman who loves his mother knows that she is always there for him; even when he didn't know, she was there. She gave him birth and fed him to become strong and healthy, and she gave him the best thing: love. With that love, he became who he is today.

The lady and the gentleman respect and love their father, because he helped them build their wings to be able to fly their own. He also taught them to overcome any weak moments they might have. The lady and the gentleman know and feel love from both parents and thank them.

The best of life's riches is knowing your value. Of course, you have to be open minded so you can learn a thing or two. Handling yourself like a lady or a gentleman is really worth it, but do it with sincerity. Love is the best feeling, so live your life with the people and the things that you love. Everything works out for the best when you are surrounded by love. All is well.

Remember Christmas mornings when you were little? The excitement before you opened your presents? The beautiful decorations on the well-decorated Christmas tree? The music and the tasty treats? Waiting to open all the gifts from Santa? There was a very happy mother and a very happy father that made it all come true. You did feel the love. Remember how you felt?

I took time off work one holiday and went on a beautiful trip with my daughter and my mother. We visited everyone we hadn't seen for a long time. Every place we visited was full of excitement, and we brought our energy. Friends and family were very glad to share new stories and remember the olds one.

We stopped at a cottage that my dad built when I was a kid. It was nice to see the lake again; it felt like I never left. Everywhere we visited, people had either a lake or a pool. My cousin had a lake, and all the kids went swimming. It was nice to see my little girl play with her cousins. It started raining, so we called the kids in to get dry and away from the rain. But they loved swimming in the lake while it was raining.

I thought, *Wow. With all the technology that we have, there are always things in nature that can't be replaced.* We felt the love from everyone we visited. The feeling of still having a great relationship with someone that you haven't seen for a long time meant a lot to me. I was still best friends with a friend I had when I was five years old. The joy my daughter had and the lovely visit my mother had with her brothers were priceless. I couldn't ask for a better vacation.

Think of what you want and then go for it.

Every chance I have, I go to church on Sunday with my mom. After church we go for brunch, which gives us a chance to catch up on each other's life. She tells me the things that she did and all of her new plans. I tell her what's new in my life.

I know my mother spent lots of time cooking and prepare everything, just like Thanksgiving dinner. She is so happy when the whole family comes over. Those precious moments are very valuable. We all cherish those happy, memorable times. We do it to feel good and to make others feel good. It makes me happy to see my mother happy. Next time you go to someone else's house for supper, remember the feeling of those who took the time to make a special moment very memorable.

Be there for your parents when they need help or any time they feel like they need your presence. Remember, you are a very big part of their lives.

I helped my mom build a deck. We both laughed, told stories and—most of all—got to know each other better. A lot of things happens in one's life, and it's fun to be able to share it with someone—especially your parents. They are always proud of you, though some parent show it and some don't. But you can show how much you appreciate them by simply being there with them.

Every mom is a supermom and every dad is a superdad. You know that your parents did a lot just to make sure you were well fed and warm. They made sure that your vehicle was a good one and reliable. If they did all that, they have done lots that you don't remember. Is it so hard to hug them and tell them you love them?

As much as we love one another, my dad and I never really said it. I was in the garage with my dad one day, and I told him, "Dad, remember when I was a little kid, and after I put on my pajamas and got ready for bed, I used to run up and give you my biggest hug? Then, when I was still a boy, I didn't do that anymore. My sisters always did; they never stopped hugging. But I stopped, because it wasn't cool." Then I said, "Dad, I love you. And from this moment I will tell you every chance I have, and I will hug you just like when I was a little kid." My father was not the type to do that but I gave him the biggest hug. I know that deep down he really liked it.

From that day on, I hugged him, and on the phone I told him that I loved him. He would not say it back, but one day he did say, "I love you," and for me that meant everything. My father passed away, and you know, my friend, I am so glad that I had that relationship with my dad.

The way you look at life is all in your attitude, your perception, your thoughts, and your beliefs. It is the way you were brought up. When I sign my name, I am proud of who I am.

Him and her

The woman (whom you already know I like to refer as a lady) and the man (or gentleman) do not kiss and tell, because it is disrespectful to do so. Period. This is true in any situation: when you respect someone, you don't do anything to hurt him or her. You do not yell at someone you respect. You are not mean to someone you love. You don't make fun of the person you care for. When you and your partner are visiting friends, please don't ever disrespect your partner in any way shape or form.

Strong women and men are strong in their emotions and make their presence count.

When you care about your friends' feelings and their self-respect, you are there for them, just as they are there for you. When there is a lack of respect in the matter, you can stop at any time. If there is no respect, you do not waste their time. It is totally not worth it for you or for you friends.

To be exceptionally honest, you have to be present at each moment—even if you are not near them. I speak from experience, because I travel for my work most of the time, but I always wanted to be there.

Ladies and gentlemen make great moms and dads, because they care. When a woman and a man are happy and care about their lives, they automatically care for others' needs and wants. Always make room for someone who cares.

Bigger is better. A big heart is big in generous actions. A gentleman is a man you want on your side. You don't want a man who does not respect other people's properties and who is needy and mean. You are a lady and you want to be around a true gentleman. A real man, in my opinion, is one who knows his priorities; he knows what is important. His partner is number one—not his buddies, not a car, not golf. A man should know this. But if he doesn't know, someone should tell him.

The person that you want to be with should love to smile and have a life. He should be able to make a life for himself. He will make your time and life worth it.

The man who brings flowers or something in that meaning, it is with great affection it is not about the item he purchased; it is the thought that counts. It is a gesture that says he thought of you and has feelings for you. He cares, and it is a way of saying, "I was thinking of you, and this is a gift to show you my gratitude and my feelings toward you. This is what you mean to me."

Invest your time in someone who is never bored and never boring. Your life is full of positivity; your life is open to all that is good and new. You will always have room for someone who cares. You want to live for today and make today better than yesterday. Focus on today.

Being surrounded by a gentleman gives you good energy; it is a great feeling to be with a positive person. You feel like you can do anything and you can, because everything that you will be doing will be with great respect for yourself.

The confident woman and the confident man have an exceptional aura that surrounds them. People are drawn to great women and great men who know who they are. You want to be with someone who is positive and has a genuine smile, because you know that all things that come into your life are because of your own doing.

There are great women and great men everywhere, but some people forget who they are because of too much ambition, too much stress, and other factors in their life, but it is just for a brief moment. Be someone that others can count on; be someone that people can trust because you say what you mean, and you are polite about it.

Do what makes you feel good, that makes you happy. Always treat yourself; in your spare time, do something that you really love doing. Just take time and enjoy your life. It is your life so you want to treat yourself well. If you don't, who will? Don't be selfish or self-centered, but if you feel like you need this time, by all means do it.

Aim high. Live and learn by your actions, not foolishly but with understanding. You have to stand tall; be proud of who you are, brushing the dirt off your knees and then walking with dignity, walking with true understanding of yourself.

When you go out for a nice meal, it's good to dress up and feel great about yourself. Most people take the time to look their best; it makes going out extra special. The whole time that you spending making yourself look good—as you put on a dress or a tie—you feel good. You do this because you really appreciate the quality time that you are having.

Wish all the people that you encounter a nice and beautiful day. Life is what you want it to be. Knowing that you made someone's day really feels great. When your life is good, you want to do more to improve it. You want to grab onto life and *live*. Be grateful for all you have accomplished.

Sign your name with confidence, because you know that you did everything to the best of your knowledge. You are beautiful simply because of your confidence, your honesty, and your respect and love for others. You indeed shake people's hands firmly, and you hug or kiss someone because you want to. You allow others to feel your true energy. You are someone with an exceptional life. You look great. Because you are being true to yourself, you are not trying to be someone that you are not. Don't waste time bragging.

Most successful people fall more than once in their life, but they know that if they get back up and brush the dirt off their knee, they will be stronger. Own up to your success just as you own up to your mistakes. Respect your boss. Know that you understand what life is about. You indeed have to live free and you have only one life. That is why it is important to live it well.

Every morning, ladies and gentlemen, say, "Thank you for a beautiful day."

If people cannot trust enough to open their heart, how can they ever experience the amazing feeling of being in love? So we continue to put our fragile hearts at risk. It's all about respect; respecting yourself and your partner means conducting yourself appropriately, whether you are in that person's presence or not.

I present myself in a way that I choose on the level I am comfortable with. Don't ever try to present anything other than your authentic self. I show the real me but only a part; not everyone gets all of me. That is my choice, based on my level of trust and comfort.

Be kind. Have faith in yourself and always believe in

yourself. Dreams do come true, so be true to those you love and be true to you.

Do not ever let fear get in your way. You created most of your fears, so you can get rid of them. When you have a dream and you truly want it, don't let fear get in the way. It will keep you from dreaming.

You are committed to your personal perfection. Make the best choices for your well-being. Create your own standard and your own improvements. Be proud of your culture. Carve your name in stone. Be elegant. Help to build your community while creating your lifestyle. Focus on what you want to become.

You are excellent in everything you do, simply because you are focused and you desire to be great. Stay on to the road of being noble. Do not put others down but own your place. Let love drive you to do well. Build your beautiful life.

You are what you think you are. To be a lady or a gentleman, you need to understand this. You want others to indulge in life. Live with a clear and healthy conscience. Be responsible for your own actions; that is why it is so important to do the best that you can. Truly be at your best.

Ladies and gentlemen love to have radiant smiles that mean life is pretty good. They are people of quality, and so are the people they know, the place they go, and the times they share. They always have their own special presence and want to feel that presence with everyone.

You give out what you want in your compliments and good actions; you live by raising the roof of your life. You have a passion to live well.

Most people want to live well and do well but we tend to forget that. It's good to get reminded and to discover something new. Follow your heart. And please be kind and generous. Love your surroundings, love yourself, and love everyone. Listen to what your heart is telling you. Have faith. Learn to trust your heart.

We all want to play. Women and men want to feel young and healthy, and to be able to play well. This is where it gets really exciting. What kind of games you are willing to play? This is where lots of great people lose and some win. Your frame of mind will determine all what is really worth. When you play with the best intentions and not with your ego—not playing just against the competition but truly playing fully with your heart—then everyone wins and wins big, especially yourself, because you made friends. Playing with noble actions will make you proud of yourself.

You have but one life, after all. All depends on what you are working toward. Only then will you know if it was worth it. It's all about priorities and what is important to you.

After all your commitment and sacrifices, you should settle for nothing less than the best with someone you really connect with. You work hard for what you want so make sure you get it.

Paint your picture of what you want but be careful what it portrays. Picture your home and your car. As far as relationship are concerned, leave it up to fate. Keep your dreams alive and keep them real. That is where real happiness truly exists.

A relationship cannot succeed without love, trust, sincerity, commitment, honesty, security, loyalty, and respect. But it all has to start with chemistry—an undeniable attraction. If you don't feel that initial attraction, how can it possibly go further?

Dream big, my friend, dream big

I really enjoyed writing this book. This is my dream, and I hope you really enjoyed reading it.

Allow me to restate the little saying I wrote in the introduction:

Joie de vivre is being entirely comfortable to be your authentic self, to be grateful and at your happiest. It involves the moments you can truly savor, knowing that you listened and trusted the love in your heart—all the love in your life. It's having full faith in yourself and being the best that you can be. It's knowing you can trust your heart to live well with the solid relationships you have established with your authentic self and with others. It's knowing you have done your absolute best. It's living with no fear and with absolute joy, going after exactly what you want, fully enjoying the journey of your life and living in the present—this very moment—because you know life is beautiful.

Just enjoy your life! Life is meant to be fun and joyful and full of love, lots of love. I know that my life *rocks*. I know what I love to do. Go ahead, have too much fun. Have faith in yourself and you will go far toward the dreams you believe in. *Make it happen.* Think of what you want and then go for it. Live your dream.

It's a good life. Take time and listen to your insides, and listen well. Life is the love that you give and the love that you receive. It's one step after another step, one smile after another. It is laughing and the crying. It is every moment that you cherish. It is the compliments you give and the compliments you received. It is the hugs and the kisses, the looks and the touches. *All of this is your life.* Your interactions with others is your life, my friend. Love everyone and surround yourself with people and things you love.

I loved writing this book; I feel alive and I am proud to be me. Hopefully this book will help you. Keep it as your daily reminder and as a boost of 100% pure energy.

Live your life to its fullest please. Be kind and proud.

Give love to everyone. That's what life is all about.

When you make a decision, follow through with it. Make it happen. Be kind.

Remember to treat others the way you would like to be treated.

Acknowledgments
"Thank you" is a sign of happiness

I just want to say with all my heart that I am so grateful for my life. Thank you so much!

I am very grateful to have a little girl, Dominique. I tell her every day that I am here to help her in life, to be here for her. My life is for her and I think she was born to help me. I thank her for really being there and making me laugh like I've never laughed before. Thank you, ma belle. Je t'aime fort et toujour.

Thank you to both of my awesome sisters, Sylvie and Michelle, for showing me what really living life is. That you to my family for always being there for me, supporting me in ways that no words can say. Thank you to my friends that gave me an unlimited supply of optimism and to every person that was there when I needed someone.

I really thank God, the Father, the maker of all; Jesus, my savior; and the Holy Spirit for guiding me for the life you have given me and for giving me a mother with enough energy to keep up with me and be the number one *maman*.

I am very grateful for such a great mother to be there when I need her in her busy life. *Merci, Maman.*

Merci, Papa, for always being there too. I know that you are always present. In every circumstance, there is a right and a wrong.

And thank you to my readers. Know that in every way you have a choice, and it is up to you to choose what is good for you. It is about how you truly feel toward the situation. Ask God to help you make the right ones.

Have a nice day! I wish you the joy of living. Joi de vivre!

And may your life be filled with all the success and happiness you deserve.

Enjoy every step of your life

About the Author

Alain was born in Ramore, a small town near Timmins (Ontario). When he was 12 years old, Alain and his family moved to Welland, located 20 minutes from Niagara Falls (Ontario). Every chance he had, he would ride his bike to "the falls" to enjoy the beautiful scenery. When Alain was 19 years old he enrolled in the Canadian military, a career he deeply enjoyed. Later, he changed his career to the oil field of Alberta Canada.

Alain has a wonderful daughter named Dominique who he is very proud of. Being well surrounded with great friends, an outstanding family and the various enriching life experiences, Alain decided to write a book about the joy of living life and how to achieve this by being kind to people. To name but a few of his qualities, Alain is very attentive to others and their needs, he is kind, generous and considerate... a true gentleman! His written thoughts in this book are reflective of his true feelings and actions; he believes that while respecting others is important, respecting yourself is crucial. He is very comfortable putting his real self forward, is confident in expressing how he truly feels inside his heart and does not believe in fear.